I0474948

MAKE LIFE WORK

PERSONAL GROWTH FOR TODAY'S ENTREPRENEUR

CREATING YOUR ONLINE BUSINESS FROM THE INSIDE OUT
IS THE ONLY REAL PATH TO SUCCESS!

MAKE LIFE WORK

PERSONAL GROWTH FOR TODAY'S ENTREPRENEUR

CREATING YOUR ONLINE BUSINESS FROM THE INSIDE OUT

IS THE ONLY REAL PATH TO SUCCESS!

~ Gemeem Davis ~

Life equals *You*, the innermost part of you. *Work* refers not to your job, but to the required power, energy and effort it takes to move you from one place to another. To *make life work* is to allow the inner *You* to release the power, energy and effort needed to move you from where you are to where *You* want to be.

DEDICATION

For *You*, the brave ones who just knew there was more to you and the creation of a successful business. Here's the answer, guidance and confirmation you've been waiting for. Contributing to your growth, success, happiness and freedom fuels me.

xoxoxo

Gemeem

CONTENTS

FORWARD

Imagine... you're about to take off on the adventure of a lifetime. You are filled with excitement and your energy is off the charts. You're absolutely beaming with anticipation about what you will do and see and who you will meet. "This is going to be a blast!" you think as you make your way through the airport check-in. However, as you approach the gate, you start feeling apprehensive and the little voice inside your head starts talking. "What are you doing? You can't take a trip like this, you've got responsibilities! You don't even know where you're going and those people, they could be dangerous. You don't even like flying. The plane might crash! Yikes!!!" Sweaty palms, you're now scared and confused. You want to take flight but at the same time fear has taken over and you want to turn back. You stand there, like you're paralyzed, contemplating what you should do.

Often, when it comes to following through on goals, people find themselves in the same predicament as the one described above, stuck somewhere between "wanting" success and "achieving" results, wondering what to do. Their initial excitement gets drowned out by incessant thinking, wrapped up in doubt and fear, disguised as "rational". When this happens, we all have a tendency to look outside ourselves for answers. We turn to coaches, trainers, consultants, family and friends to lead and motivate us. After spending a long time in that in-between space, I've learned it's a waste of time to look to others. The answers are inside of you and only you.

Make Life Work gives you the answers that are inside of you. By guiding you through the most important conversation you will ever have, the one between you and *You*. The physical you and the innermost part of you. I call this, *The Great Conversation* and when you actively engage it you will open the door to all that is. You won't need to be motivated because you will be inspired by your own clarity. Your clarity will then pick you up and move you out of "wanting". You will have direction.

Clarity, choice and action, this is the way to make life work. Everyone that you admire has followed these same steps, all the true Internet marketing "gurus" like Jeff Walker, Eben Pagan, and Frank Kern to personal development leaders, T. Harv Eker, and Jack Canfield. All your famous entertainers, athletes and money makers like Oprah, Trump and Warren Buffet use it too. They've used these steps because this is the only way, to get you from where you are to where you want to be. Ahh, the sweet taste of success.

Embrace it and be on your way.

I spent a lot of time in the airport.

When I decided to start my business I was really *really* excited about the possibilities of more freedom, money and the opportunity to positively impact people's lives. I knew I had great information to share and was eager to do so. Having the great fortune of awareness, I knew exactly how "the secret", law of attraction, was working in my life, how I had attracted what I wanted *and* what I did *not* want. My business was to be the vehicle that allowed me to fully engage the life I was dreaming about, consistently being of service to others as opposed to just touching that dream from time to time, coming in and out of "success".

In my transition from employee to small business owner, I thought I would be creating an offline personal and professional development training company. I set up a website, kicked off my business with a free seminar in my hometown, got my first professional contract, did a private consultation and gave a talk to a group of travel agents. Everybody loved what I had to say. I was building momentum.

The idea was to model my business after personal growth powerhouses I respected, namely Jack Canfield and T. Harv Eker. Studying what they were doing, I realized they were both very active selling their products and services online. Something I knew absolutely nothing about.

So what did I do? I got busy trying to figure out how to market myself and make money online. That's when I got stuck in my "online airport".

I was receiving so much information, so quickly, from so many online marketing "experts" that I got confused. My fear about not knowing, doing things wrong and the technical aspects of being a solo-entrepreneur with a home-based business was paralyzing. Before I knew it, I didn't even know what business I was in anymore. Was I an Internet marketer, life coach, business consultant, personal growth trainer, keynote speaker, author? Should I be an affiliate or get affiliates? Should I publish a newsletter or blog, be on Facebook or Twitter, pay for advertising to generate traffic to my site, or focus on article marketing, video marketing or do tele-seminars? Was I going to do live events or virtual webinars? Every expert claimed their way was the best way. I didn't have a clue. Can you say *information overload*?

The noise on the Internet was clouding my vision and my response was typical. I procrastinated. And, when I did muster up the energy to make a move, my actions did not produce the results I wanted.

Can you relate?

After spending months wandering around my "online airport", wasting time and money, it became imperative that I make a move. Not an outward or forward move to the latest, greatest, hyped up, get rich on the Internet move. No, I knew I needed to travel inward.

I went on a personal growth retreat. For five full days, I did not check my email, work on my website, contact a colleague, write an article or update my Facebook status. I got in touch with me and was reminded that the "soul" purpose for my business is to help people all over the world live life on their terms with confidence, freedom and joy! The information you will find in <u>Make Life Work</u>, helps you to do that. I have been a student and practitioner of this information in some way, shape or form for the past fifteen years. And with this publication, the student (that would be me :-) has now become the teacher. Teaching what she most needs to *continue* learning.

This is not a "how to make real money online" book that you can read in a day, toss to the side and do nothing with. It is a *workbook* that calls on you to engage the material, processes and principles of transformation and success. As an entrepreneur it may very well be the most important tool you'll use to create the lifestyle and business that you know you are capable of creating.

I like to think of the documents you will produce from the work you do here as your *Personal Declaration of Independence*, your founding documents. It is the master plan that comes before you write your official business plan.

I'm glad I had this information as part of my "blueprint". It allowed me to quiet the noise in my "airport", focus on my takeoff and fly. I'm confident you will do the same!

Now, let's get to work!

One of the biggest mistakes solo entrepreneurs make is thinking they can do everything by themselves. Nobody does anything without support. Find you some and success will be yours.

~Gemeem~

ACKNOWLEDGMENTS

My heart is filled with gratitude for every single person, book, movie and/or video that gently led me to allowing <u>Make Life Work</u> to come forward. I am particularly grateful to the Franklin Covey trainer (I can't remember her name) who introduced me to the concept and principles of living a value based life nearly fifteen years ago. To the Creative Capital Foundation for allowing me to coordinate one of the best professional development workshop programs for artists in the country and step right into fulfilling "my promise". Thank you to my dear friends and colleagues, Colleen Keegan, for giving me my first experience leading a workshop and who read my first proposal and drafts and said "Yes, I think it's a fabulous idea to start your own business!", and Esther Robinson, filmmaker and founder of Art Home, your friendship means the world to me. Thanks for sending me "love" at exactly the right moments. We are changing the world!

Thank you to Sandra Salvato, The former Director of Professional Development at Gullivers Travel Associates (New York) for reminding me, I always have to *give my best*. You are an awesome trainer. A special thanks go out to Erika Kendrick for introducing me to the idea of self publishing through her Publishing Prep seminar. Thank you to Ty Cohen for inviting me to do my first tele-seminar.

Thank you so very much to my oldest and bestest friend, Marsha "Nikki" Dorsey, aka my M & M! Love you girl. Thank you to my brothers, Andre Melvin, Joshua Melvin aka Johnny Voltik and Joseph Davis, "C'mon we have to bond!" Joan, love you and the kids, Avery, Grace and Ellis, what an awesome family I have! Thank you to my friend, Mashhur Anam, "Let's meet at Barnes & Noble", our talks feed my soul. To my soul sistah, Demetra Baylor, "We eagles fly together!" Thank you for being here, for the awesome cover design and doing all the things I had no clue how to do. Love you much.

I am also so very grateful for Marie Diamond, Annette Rugolo and the entire staff at Learning Strategies, the retreat and seminars I took with you all opened me up in a way I could never have imagined. My time spent in Minnesota, and on the tele-seminars inspired me to finish writing, <u>Make Life Work</u>. I am so grateful!

And last but certainly not least, I want to say thank you to Ms. Maggie Gill, my mother, my friend, confidant, biggest fan, and proof reader, I love you more than words can say. <u>Make Life Work</u> would not be possible if not for you. "OK Mama!" (in my most annoying voice =)

INTRODUCTION

I am overjoyed that you have connected with me and <u>Make Life Work!</u> It doesn't matter how the connection occurred. Whether you purchased the book by itself, signed up for the 4-Week Course or got a copy from a friend, the most important thing is that you are here, and I am delighted!

The main objective of <u>Make Life Work</u> is to give you "practicable" information, tools and support so that you will be inspired and empowered to take action - to move - in the direction of what you want, your hopes, your dreams, and your goals.

For many of you that dream is to have a successful online business. Believe me, I know. In fact; I'm just like you in that regard. We all want to tell our success story of how we transformed our lives and made a butt load of cash on the Internet!

The good news is that there are tons of programs on the market to help you make that happen. You know, they're the "how to find your niche, choose your market, capture leads, generate traffic, create a marketing funnel and do product launches" type of programs. Those are all great and you will need to utilize *some* of them in due time. Just not right now. Not when you are just starting out or restructuring your business. Here's the reason why.

A lot of those programs, the people who create and promote them, as well as the people that buy them sometimes forget that the key component to success is *You*. That real success is an inside job. So the first logical step to creating any successful business is to take some time focusing on *You*.

<u>Make Life Work</u> is your golden opportunity to engage with *You*, to tap into the power of real success. So that whatever effort you put into building your business *works* to deliver you your desired results.

What you experience in life, your business, relationships, health, and your finances are the results of your dominant beliefs, feelings and habits. To get what you really want it is imperative that you become aware of what those beliefs, feelings and habits are *communicating to you*.

<u>Make Life Work</u> has been designed to facilitate that communication effectively. It is, *The Great Conversation* between you and *You*, the physical you and the within *You*. Through your conscious awareness of it you will come to understand, *where you're coming from*, which is critical to transforming your life and creating your business.

It's spiritual work based in a business practice or vice versa…

The <u>Make Life Work</u> process is in part based on a simple business practice known as *strategic planning*. Strategic Planning is an organizations way of defining who they are, what their objectives are and how they will achieve them. To do that, they follow the three step SEE, DRAW, & THINK/MAP process.

Businesses SEE where they are by conducting a SWOT (strengths, weaknesses, opportunities and threats) analysis. DRAW where they want to be by developing vision/mission statements. Then, THINK or MAP how to get there by creating S.M.A.R.T. business objectives.

<u>Make Life Work</u> simply adapts that process to meet the needs of *today's entrepreneurs*, online and home-based business owners.

With <u>Make Life Work</u> you will:

✔ Engage The Great Conversation by exploring the *Language of Life*, expanding your awareness of who *You* are and making an assessment of the *7 Key Indicators of Where You Are*, in your body, relationships, appearance, environment, business, time and finances, to truly SEE who and where you are.

✔ Frame Your Great Conversation by creating a vision for your life and business based on *what you have to give*. Through your *Personal Statement of Purpose*, your *Soul's Purpose* and *Business Mission Statement*, you will DRAW where you want to be.

✔ Focus Your Great Conversation by creating *B.I.G. S.M.A.R.T.* Goals. Bold Intentions of Gratitude that are Specific, Measurable, Attainable, Relevant and Timely, effectively putting more details on your DRAWING.

✔ Master Your Great Conversation. Concentrating on what needs to change on the inside, so what you really want shows up on the outside, you'll THINK or MAP your way to success. You will create powerful affirmations, learn a very simple meditation and consciously incorporate new habits into your life that allow you to tap into your abundant *Having Space*. In a nutshell you'll change your mind-set and your heart-set.

EXPLORING THE LANGUAGE OF LIFE

Life speaks. The language it uses to communicate are your thoughts, feelings and emotions. The circumstances in your life, what you have and don't have are the results of this ongoing, all inclusive *Great Conversation*. Consciously engaging, framing, focusing and mastering your Great Conversation is what will make your life and your business a success. To begin the process, it's imperative that you become aware of the conversation you've been having with *Yourself*, i.e. Life, the Universe, God up until now. Your first step, expand your vision of who you think *You* are.

Are you stuck on the "Think & Do" you?

I love, appreciate and am very proud to be a part of the self-help/personal growth industry. The very idea of my work positively impacting people and the world is the fuel that led me to put pen to paper and write <u>Make Life Work</u>. However, in my study and experience as a personal growth expert, I've noticed an alarming trend. The self-help industry seems to be stuck on the "think & do" you, that is your physical body and your mind. Everywhere you turn the marketing message is the same. Think positive, change your mind-set and the *doing you* will take care of everything. You'll be successful. Now, there's nothing really wrong with that except it's only half true. Don't you think positive? Don't you work towards your goals? The reason that's only half true and why you subsequently don't see all the success you've been *thinking* about is because you're only using half of your creative faculties.

Believe it or not there is more to you than your physical body and your mind. You also have an emotional and spiritual body and they both play just as much a role in your success as what your *think & do* self does.

The knowledge that your emotional and spiritual bodies, the lighter side of you, are integral parts of the creative process have generally gone missing from traditional business material. There are many reasons for this however these three seem to be the most pervasive.

First, owning a business has traditionally been about imposing one's will on others. It was the exchange of money for a physical product. The hard sell and persuasive marketing strategies were born out of this intention to get people to buy regardless of need and/or genuine want. In fact, false needs were (and still are) created through advertising for the sole purpose of convincing people to purchase whatever was being sold.

Second, even though executives at the very top levels in business have known that there is more to creating real success than could be seen, many fear that any public acknowledgement of that truth could lead to a loss of control and power over their employees, customers and competition. So the information has been kept hidden, a secret only for a chosen few. Talk about universal principles and the law of attraction are avoided as not to be misconstrued or used by the people they seek to control. Instead, the *energy* of a company is discussed in terms of morale and personal growth teachings are sold as professional development, often disguised as management training. It's just been easier and more profitable for executives to focus on the *think & do* you and play along with the false premise that "if it can't be measured, it doesn't exist".

And third, people falsely believe that by working *only* with the mind you have a short cut to creating what you want. It is easy to see why this is so because there is validity to the phrase, "change your mind, change your life". Our brain, which is the physical representation of our mind, is where we form habits. What we habitually do becomes our reality. However the mind can be quite illusive. That's why working solely with the mind doesn't work. In order to be successful you need to anchor what you want in your *subconscious* higher self. If you don't you'll probably be thinking positive and saying affirmations for a very long time without getting the results you want. But you already knew that, right?

Business executives have been in the practice of manipulating the subconscious minds of others for a very long time. But thankfully, times are changing and a more comprehensive understanding of success and new ways of doing business are now coming forth. Hence, <u>Make Life Work: Personal Growth For Today's Entrepreneur</u> has been born.

The Universe recognizes vibration. Vibration (according to one definition in the dictionary) is a distinctive, *emotional atmosphere* capable of being sensed. Anchoring your desires in your subconscious mind requires *openness* to your personal emotional atmosphere, that is your emotional body. Your feelings, what you emote, are the *language of life*. They are your sensing mechanism. They are what you use to communicate with the *You* that is your higher self. What you're feeling is the *content* or *substance* of your true wants, prayers and requests to the Universe. They are glaring signposts telling you where you are and pointing you in a *certain* direction. Therefore, you're not where you *say* you are. You're where you *feel* you are. Opening up to your emotional body is the act of paying attention to your feelings and discerning their messages without judgement. This is the work of an enlightened entrepreneur and how you master your Great Conversation.

I know from my own past experience that "figuring out" what your feelings are telling you can seem like a daunting task. The good news is that in the context of the Great Conversation, there is no "figuring out" involved. The only thing you need to be concerned with is whether your emotions are leading you towards what you want or away from what you want. When you get your answer, accept what is, then make a conscious decision (if you feel you are in a bad, negative, unwanted emotional place) to get to a better feeling place. Better feeling places are ones of hope, gratitude, courage, happiness, joy, celebration and love.

For example, one of my goals is to have a successful personal growth company with a massive online presence. When I checked into my feelings about that, I realized I was feeling overwhelmed and fearful that the task was too great. For a while, I let that feeling dictate my behavior. I procrastinated a lot. To turn things around, I had to get to my better feeling place of hope and courage. The minute I got to hope, which incidentally came after I attended a personal growth retreat, I started work on completing this book. I still procrastinate sometimes, but I'm no longer paralyzed by fear.

By suggesting that you pay attention and discern what your feelings are communicating to you, I am in no way advocating that you start living completely from your emotional body. Your emotional body can be just as precarious as your mind. To cultivate success from the inside out, simply accept that all parts of *You* make up a magnificent whole that must be understood, respected and honored.

Business in the past was about the exchange of money for a physical product. Today it's about the exchange of money for information. Information is not tangible. It is a string of thoughts put together in a certain way for a specific purpose. It is *light*.

Increasingly our information is coming from the ether, in digital format. The Internet has made it so that we no longer have to physically go anywhere to buy a product. We simply click a button and the information we want instantly appears, like magic. In that exchange, what we're actually receiving are simply *patterns of light*, pixels or dots of color that when coded a certain way appear familiar to us, on our computer screens. Looking at it from that perspective, one could say that the Internet is literally allowing us to move away from the density of our physical form in the direction of light or spirit, opening the door for magic to appear in our lives, for acceptance of the non-physical *working* on our behalf. How cool is that?

This is a great opportunity for solo entrepreneurs, Internet marketers, home based business owners or really anybody looking to engage the information age and make money online. All that is required is your willingness to play with the non-physical, its principles and processes and master the *light* that's inside of you. Begin by becoming intimate with the non-physical parts of *You*.

It's time to go beyond the mind and body.

HOW TO "SEE" YOU

There is more to you than your physical body and your mind. You have a physical, mental, spiritual and emotional body. Together these bodies represent the foundational aspects of who *You* are. You can think of your emotional, mental and spiritual bodies as circles of energy around your physical body. Lots of people refer to these energies as your aura or vibe.

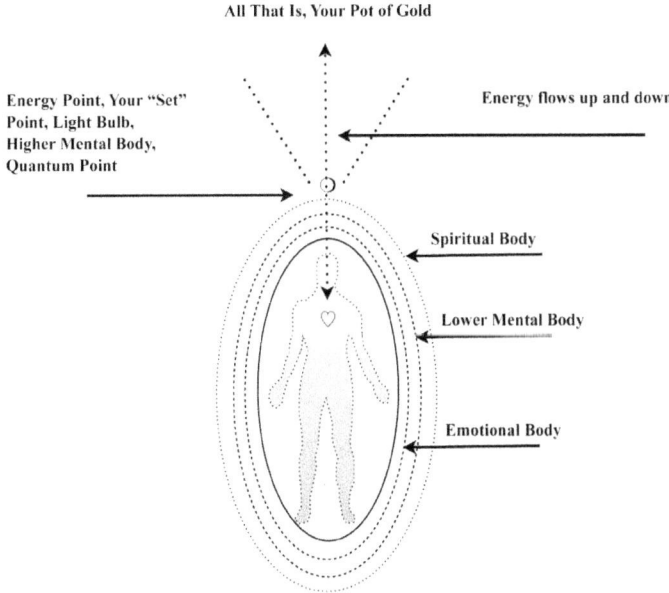

THE ASPECTS OF YOU

Your Spiritual Body:

Your spiritual body is the lightest and most receptive part of you. At the top of your spiritual body is a point of light, a magnetic energy point that pulls divine inspiration, ideas etc., down from the Universe and fills your spiritual body up with it. When you are conscious of this pulling down of inspiration you have a "light bulb" or "aha" moment.

Your Lower Mental Body:

I like to think of the Lower Mental Body or mind, as a transformational or processing energy center. It is the place in you that takes your inspiration and begins grounding it into your physical experience. It has no filter and simply responds to whatever inspired it, immediately creating or accessing the mental programs (thoughts) and physical programs (habits) it needs to manifest your inspiration into the world. It acts like a bridge between the lighter side of you (spirit and emotions) and the densest part of you (physical body).

Your Emotional Body:

Your emotional body is your "feeling body". Think of it as your "chief communicator". As your spiritual body receives inspiration and your lower mental body transforms that inspiration into thought forms (thoughts becomes things, right?) it sends an instant message to your emotional body and you begin emoting feelings. When you are in balance and accept the message, what your spiritual body has already given you and your mental body has already "made so" you generate positive emotions (joy, love, excitement, peace, gratitude.) and feel good. When you are out of alignment and are resisting the messages, you generate negative emotions (fear, doubt, jealousy, etc.) and feel bad. Your feelings will always tell you "where you are" on any given subject or situation in your life. They let you know where your spirit has already taken you. Note: No emotion is really bad. It is what it is, simply a message.

Your Physical Body:

Your physical body which is your giving/action center is the densest part of *You*. As you receive inspiration, thoughts or mental programs and feelings on any particular subject, they are deposited in your physical body at your heart center. From your heart you begin radiating the light of what's inside of you, what you already have, your ideas, thoughts, and feelings. This is how you authentically give to others. Your body, which runs entirely on automatic (you don't think about breathing, walking, moving a limb) has no choice but to move into action based on the messages it has received from your spiritual, mental and emotional bodies. Your physical body is therefore simply a tool or the vehicle that moves your spirit into form.

You are more than what you see.

As an entrepreneur, I know you've heard of the concept of effortless success. Accessing and consciously utilizing the different aspects of *You* is the key to that process and moving yourself out of *wanting* and into *having* the results you wish for.

It is also the key to "finding" your niche. When you start with *You*, what you'll find is that there is no real need to find a niche. When you start with *You*, you'll attract your perfect niche and create and/or sell information products and programs that are aligned with the core of who you are and resonate with people looking for what you have to offer. The need to use overly persuasive and disingenuous marketing strategies for the express purpose of making money will cease to be an issue for you.

Throughout <u>Make Life Work</u>, you will have the opportunity to practice accessing the non-physical aspects of *You* at the end of each section as an Inner Work meditation exercise. Be easy with this. There is no right or wrong way to meditate. All that you'll be doing is sitting quietly.

Now, staying in the awareness that you are *more*, you can begin consciously engaging *The Great Conversation* about where you are.

SELF ASSESSMENT

Where you are is how you feel.

You are the foundation from which you are building your business. Get clear on *all* of you. As a solo entrepreneur, it's important that you begin consciously engaging *Your Great Conversation* by making an assessment of the *7 Key Indicators of Where You Are*, in your body, relationships, appearance, environment, business, finances, and time. Your assessment is done not so you can dwell in your results, but so you can move forward with clarity and confidence.

Whether conscious of it or not, you've been engaged in *The Great Conversation* since the day you were born. The circumstances, things and people around you are proof of it. If you want greater insight into what you've been talking about or want to know the quality of your conversation, all you have to do is take a quick look at the results you're currently living with.

In your notebook answer the following questions. No, you do not have to answer every single question for each one of the 7 Keys. You may even choose not to answer any of them and simply reflect on the topic and journal your feelings. Knowing what you now know about your emotional body and its role as chief communicator, pay attention to where you feel resistance, hesitancy, frustration, stuck, at a loss for words, etc., that's your indication of where you are and that your spirit wants you to move to a "good" place, mentally and physically. If you're already feeling good, great!

Have fun with this!

What is your body communicating to you?

What is your age, height and weight?

What do you like about your body?

What's your best feature?

How old do you feel?

Do you hide your age?

Do you have aches and pains? Where and how often?

Do you exercise on a regular basis?

How many times a year do you catch a cold?

Do you have a chronic illness or condition?

Are you tired a lot or do you have an abundance of energy?

Do you avoid going to the Doctor for routine check-ups?

On a scale from 1 to 10 rate how happy you are with your body.

What are your relationships communicating to you?

What is your relationship status?

Besides you, who's the most important person or persons in your life?

Have you communicated how much you love them to them?

Describe your relationships with your co-workers.

Do you have old friends/lasting friendships? How long?

How often do you laugh? What are you laughing at or about?

Do you feel like you are free to be yourself?

How do you express yourself around other people? Are you the life of the party, loud, quiet, shy, timid, funny?

Are you open to other people's opinions and experiences?

Do you have people in your life you can trust?

Are you a trustworthy friend?

When you get together with your family and friends is your conversation full of gossip or "venting" about other people?

Do your family and friends treat you the way you want to be treated?

Are you in conflict or fighting with anyone?

How do you show love and support to others?

Do you feel like you could use more friends, different friends?

On a scale from 1 to 10 rate how happy you are with your current relationships.

What are you communicating through your appearance?

Describe your personal style. Are you chic, streamlined, conservative, punk, goth, hippie, hip hop, provocative?

Is your wardrobe and hairstyle current or have you had the same style for years?

Do you wear clothes that fit and flatter your body?

Do you always "have nothing to wear"?

Are you dressing for the job you have now or the job you want?

Would you say you project a neat, clean, well put together you?

Open your closet and look at your clothes and shoes. Notice anything? Are all of your clothes the same color, style? Are they old or new (still got the tags on them)?

Are you hiding behind your appearance, wearing baggy, unflattering clothes or being extreme?

Can you go out of the house without your makeup on?

Do you always have to look your best?

Do you go broke, buying clothes you can't afford?

On a scale from 1 to 10 rate how happy you are with your appearance.

What is your environment communicating to you?

What neighborhood, City, State, and Country do you live in?

Describe where you live. Is it conservative, progressive, laid back, a college town, quiet, noisy, peaceful, friendly, at war, crime ridden, rodent and/or bug infested?

Why have you chosen to live there?

Do you think your home and/or office represents you? How?

Is your home and work environment clean?

How do you feel when you walk into your space?

Is your space small, cluttered, spacious, well organized, beautiful, junkie, etc.?

Look around your home and office. What colors are in your space?

Do you like what you see?

Do you like or love your space?

Do you feel comfortable there?

On a scale from 1 to 10 rate how happy you are with your current environment and living situation.

What is your business communicating to you?

(These questions take into account that many online entrepreneurs have 9 to 5's).

What inspired you to start your business?

How are you adding value to people's lives?

Are you making any money in your business?

Are you looking to make a quick buck or are you interested in building a viable business?

Other than paying you a salary how does your work impact your life and your family?

Are there opportunities to advance?

Who are you partnering with? Are you in win/win partnerships?

What aspects of your business do you like the most and least?

List your strengths and weaknesses.

Do you use your skills and talents in your current position?

Do you dread Mondays and live for Fridays?

Describe your relationship with your boss and co-workers.

What if anything would you do if you didn't have to work?

Are you keeping your current job because of the benefits?

Are you excited about what you do?

On a scale from 1 to 10 rate how happy you are with the current state of your business.

SEVEN DAY TRACKING EXERCISE

Interestingly, how people think about and spend their money is often reflected in how they think about and spend their time. In your notebook, for seven consecutive days track your financial and time expenditures. Note what you're doing and how long it took to complete a task. Record your predominate thoughts about money and time at the end of each day.

Consider the following "money" questions

How much money do you have in your wallet right now?

What is your take home salary per week/month/year?

Do you balance your bank accounts every week/month?

Do you receive money from multiple sources?

Do you live paycheck to paycheck?

Do you feel like you need to make more money?

Do you donate money to causes you care about on a regular basis?

Do you have debt? How much? Who do you owe?

Do you dread opening your bills?

Do you pay your bills on time or are you always coming up short?

Are you a saver, spender, thrifty, a tightwad or just really responsible?

Do you have enough money to meet all of your needs?

Do you worry about money?

When you have cash are you quick to spend it?

Are you inclined to say out loud or to yourself that you can/cannot afford something?

On a scale from 1 to 10 rate how happy you are with your current financial situation.

Consider the following "time" questions

Do you value time?

How do you show whether you value it or not?

What time do you normally get up in the morning?

Are you always running to catch a subway, train, bus or speeding in your car?

How much time did you spend watching television, preparing meals, cleaning?

Did you do the same things today as you did yesterday?

Did you have fun today? What did you do?

Do you believe time is money?

How much time did you spend working on your business today?

What did you do? Did you complete a task?

How much time did you spend on Facebook, Twitter or any other social networking site?

How many times did you check your email today?

How much time did you give yourself today?

Did you spend any time reading or working on your personal and/or professional growth?

Do you feel guilty about wanting a little alone time?

On a scale from 1 to 10 rate how happy you are with your current time management skills.

FINANCIAL FREEDOM

Let's face it!

One of the greatest motivators for starting a home based business is the potential for financial freedom. While many people romanticize this idea with being able to buy expensive big ticket items, taking lavish vacations and the ability to never have to work for "the man" ever again, you should know that chasing after financial freedom will only lend itself to the need to keep chasing after it. You already have financial freedom. You make choices every day about what to do or NOT to do with your money... no matter how much or how little you think you have.

Look at the choices you've made. Gather up all your financial documents, your bills, bank account statements, retirement statements, life insurance policies, etc. Make a list of all your outstanding financial obligations. Then, make another list of how much money you have. Be grateful for what you see. It is what it is. And you certainly have the freedom and power to change any circumstance. Make a separate list for business assets and expenses as well.

Keep it simple. You don't have to make an elaborate spreadsheet filled with categories and subcategories. Just take a piece of paper and make a few columns. See the examples on the following page. Of course, it's cool if you already have that detailed spreadsheet =).

Example #1:

Financial Obligation	Outstanding Balance	Monthly Payment
Mortgage/Rent	N/A	$1,200.00
Credit Card	$2,354.97	$60.00
Student Loan	$25,000.00	$275.00

Example #2:

What I Have Now	Balance
Checking	$998.75
Savings	$2,000.73
IRA	$5,397.51

WHERE YOU ARE

Assessment Statements

After you've answered the assessment questions and completed the *Seven Day Tracking and Financial Freedom* exercises, make an assessment of where you are for each of the 7 Key Indicators. Remember, where you are is how you feel. Are you in a good place? Are you at peace, ambivalent, in conflict, crisis or turmoil? Are you happy? In your assessment, state where you are physically, mentally and emotionally.

For example, your physical position with regards to money may be that you are rich. However, it's possible that you are in a bad way about that emotionally, indicating you're *not* headed in the right direction. Alternatively, you may be broke but be in a good emotional place indicating your *are* headed in the right direction.

Your Body

_____

_____

_____

_____

_____

_____

_____

Your Appearance

_____

_____

_____

_____

_____

Your Relationships

_____

_____

_____

_____

Your Environment

_____

_____

_____

_____

_____

Your Business

_____

_____

_____

_____

_____

Your Finances

_____

_____

_____

_____

_____

Your Time

_____

_____

_____

_____

_____

WHAT'S GOOD?

Reframe where you are

The objective of your self assessment was to increase your awareness. However, where you are does not have to dictate where you'll end up in your future. Remember, you have the power to change any circumstance in your life. Besides, when your start focusing *Your Great Conversation* using B.I.G. S.M.A.R.T. goals you can choose to consciously set a goal that represents where you want to be for each of the 7 Keys.

Awareness is simply an openness to what is. When you are open you can release the issues, circumstances and mental programs that created the unwanted things in your life. <u>Make Life Work</u> at its core is about recognizing that you are far more than what you see and experience. Your willingness to be open to that is what will allow positive change to flow into your life.

Open up to the possibility that *everything is all good*. When you want to start anything, cspccially a ncw busincss you want to build that business on a solid foundation. You want to feel good. For many people, looking honestly at their present circumstances makes them feel bad or less than because seeing what they actually have *or* don't have, doesn't match up to their mental image of themselves in comparison to others. Staying there, wrapped up in the bad, will only produce more bad.

Reframe where you are. See things differently.

You get to decide what has meaning in your life. You can choose to look and feel that your past and present circumstances are proof of failure, unworthiness, bad luck, unfairness, injustice, the results of a bad economy, or you can reframe what you see and shine a positive light on them. In my opinion, when you choose to see things in a positive light, you are intending to build your life on a solid foundation and new opportunities will open up for you.

Revisit your self assessment statements. If you've found that you are in a bad place for any of the 7 Keys, go back and shine a positive light on them. Look for the good, the benefit to you and/or others. Look for the lessons learned. Focusing on what's good will produce more good. If you honestly can't find something good, use your imagination and make something up!

Have fun with this!

Write a "What's Good" Statement for each of the 7 Keys

Your Body

_____

_____

_____

_____

_____

_____

_____

Your Appearance

_____

_____

_____

_____

_____

_____

Your Relationships

_____

_____

_____

_____

_____

Your Environment

_____

_____

_____

_____

_____

Your Business

_____

_____

_____

_____

_____

Your Finances

_____

_____

_____

_____

_____

_____

_____

_____

Your Time

_____

_____

_____

_____

_____

_____

_____

_____

EXPLORING THE LANGUAGE OF LIFE: INNER WORK & ACTION STEPS

Congratulations on completing your <u>Make Life Work</u> assessment. There's no learning without doing. To that end, I invite you to do the following Inner Work and Outer Work Action Steps.

INNER WORK

Take some time off. Preferably twice a day, turn off your TV, radio, computer, cell phone, Ipod, all things electronic and do nothing. Trust me you will survive this!

Relax and breathe. From your heart center imagine a beam of white light connecting you to the energy point above your head, this is your higher mental body, the point where you have direct contact with *You*, your spirit. (See the *How to "See" You* diagram). Connect in with that point and hold your attention there for as long as you can. For now, don't ask for anything, just observe what comes up for you. When you are ready, jot down your observations in your notebook.

OUTER WORK ACTION STEPS

If you haven't done so as already, answer the *Assessment Questions*, do the *Seven Day Tracking* and *Financial Freedom* exercises. Write your *Where You Are Assessment* and *What's Good* statements.

Additionally, if you have any clutter or disorganization in your home or office clear it out. Throw away things you no longer use or like. Keep only things you love, that are of value to you and represent what is good in your life now and what you want to achieve.

GO A LITTLE FURTHER

Read the article, <u>Bring Only What You Love</u> (included in the Resource section) then create your "Wall of Success".

Any questions? Email me at gemeem@makelifeworknow.com.

FRAMING YOUR GREAT CONVERSATION

Now that you've expanded your vision of who you are and consciously engaged *The Great Conversation*, it's time to shift your awareness to where you want to be. In a strategic plan, businesses frame where they want to be through the articulation of a vision and/or mission statement. A vision statement defines an organizations long term view of how they want to be perceived and operate in the world. It expresses the hopes and dreams or heart of an organization.

A mission statement is generally shorter in length than a vision statement and the good ones, in my opinion are born out of an organizations vision. It is a concise, written statement that defines the overall objective of the company and acts as a guideline for decision making and the allocation of resources. In essence is says, this is *why* we exist and we have decided to work within this particular framework - within these specific parameters.

In <u>Make Life Work</u>, your *Personal Statement of Purpose* equates to your vision statement. It is how you will begin framing your conversation with your higher self. Through it, you will express your hopes, dreams and aspirations for your life, how you see yourself moving through the world. From that view you will be able to bring forward your *Soul's Purpose* and Business Mission statement...easily.

Yes, you did read that right. I said your soul's purpose, not your life's purpose. Why? The answer is two fold. For one, I recently had an epiphany and realized that there's just too much anxiety and pressure around "finding" one's life's purpose. Which, if you understand the law of attraction, you know that all that finding and looking for your purpose only keeps you locked in the vibration of finding and looking and never actually discovering it. The second is that, defining one's life purpose has become synonymous with the *need* to define "what you want".

Wanting keeps you wanting and stops you from moving forward. Wanting keeps you rooted in the mentality and experience of *lack*. To get where you want to be you must free yourself from lack, which may be hardwired in your system and causing you to obsess about *what you want*. Furthermore, incessant wanting keeps you focused on consuming. Consuming or receiving is not bad but it is fundamentally passive. Success requires balance. Balance your receiving with *giving*.

Your ego *wants* but your soul *has*. It's time to transform the habit of asking for what you want to sharing *what you have to give*. The enlightened entrepreneur (that would be you) is shifting to this new consciousness. When you begin to believe from the core of your being that you have more than enough to meet your needs (abundance) and you are not afraid to share that which you have (giving), you can begin to shift from lack to abundance, from enslavement and its subsequent paralysis to true freedom and advancement.

As you begin creating a vision for your life and your business and expressing it in your *Personal Statement of Purpose*, your *Soul Purpose Statement* and *Business Mission* remember this basic truth. *Freedom is the absolute foundation from which you create your life and happiness is your only true goal*...really. Translating the ideals of freedom and happiness into tangible life experiences is the work you are doing, here and now.

There are three basic questions I've used throughout the years to tap into my authentic vision and open up to my soul's purpose. They are:

What do I have to give?
What's my legacy?
What does my ideal life look like?

What do I have to give?

To create a vision for your life centered around what you have to give, start with listing your gifts, talents, interest, and skills, the things you do well and are known for.

For example, everybody who knows me, knows that I love a good conversation... I started talking early, my mother said I spoke my first words when I was only 9 months old. As a child I was affectionately called "motor mouth." Adults would scold me because I had "too much mouth" and warned that my mouth was "gonna get me in trouble." In high school my favorite subject was English. I loved learning new vocabulary words. I like to read. I've noticed that when I speak, people listen. People come to me for advice. I have been told that I have a nice speaking voice. A women who barely knew me, saw my mother in a grocery store one day and said she had been praying for me, "your daughter has a voice in this world."

Is it any wonder that I've chosen to use my voice, my gift and love of communication to center my life and business around? This is not an accident folks! Answer, What do I have to give? in your notebook.

What's my legacy?

What you do, the actions you take, become your legacy. Consider this.

Alfred Noble invented dynamite in 1866 and amassed a great amount of monetary wealth from his invention. When his brother died a newspaper mistakenly published an obituary for Alfred that ran with the headline:

"The Merchant of Death is Dead: Dr. Alfred Noble who became rich by finding ways to kill more people faster than ever before died yesterday".

As a result of that premature obituary Alfred Nobel decided to take charge of his legacy. He then made a promise that his money would be used for the greater good of humanity. A foundation was established to award annual prizes in chemistry, physics, and literature and efforts towards international peace. Today, The Nobel Peace Prize is one of the world's most prestigious awards.

How would you change your life if you woke up one morning and saw your obituary in the paper? What would it say? More importantly, what do you want it to say?

Begin with the end in mind and ask yourself, what's my legacy? What lasting impression do you want to make on the world? Duplicate Dr. Alfred Nobel's experience and write your obituary or eulogy in your notebook.

What does my ideal life look like?

The very first vision clarifying exercise I did was to *imagine my ideal life*. That was fifteen years ago. This exercise was so much fun and so very freeing for me, because until that point I had never thought about the *bigness* of what my life could be (outside of daydreaming about being a famous actress or singer), never mind the fact that I had the freedom to choose how I wanted to live or that I had the power within me to make my vision a reality. The exercise was simply enough. Relax and let your mind go. Then, write it down.

Try it, you may be astonished at what comes up!

Once you've answered one or all three of the vision clarifying questions you will have a good idea about why you are here, what your soul wants to express through you. Look over your answers and pull out the essence of what is there. Then take a piece of paper and title it, *My Personal Statement of Purpose*. Write a few paragraphs or a few pages laying out your vision.

Your Soul's Purpose & Business Mission Statements

Writing your Soul Purpose and Business Mission statements from your vision is the first step in transforming that vision from the invisible world of thought and imagination to the real world, here and now. Your soul purpose and business mission statements are condensed, succinct, versions of your vision, written in a way that points to the action you will take to make your vision a reality.

To write both your soul's purpose and business mission statements look through your Personal Statement of Purpose for whatever is the predominant gift, talent, or interest you have and what action you intend to take with it. For example after doing the vision clearing exercises and writing my Personal Statement of Purpose, I could see very clearly that communication, expressing myself was most important to me. It is my gift I can give to the world. Examples of my soul's purpose and business mission statements are on page 38.

As a solo entrepreneur you may find that you don't need to have a business mission statement that's completely different from your soul's purpose statement. However you should be able to translate your purpose into a clear mission for your business. For example if your soul purpose is to "bring laughter to millions" your businesses mission can be an extension of that and be articulated as, "I bring joy to millions by supplying people with information and products that use humor to teach life lessons."

With your vision, purpose and mission in place you have direction. Now, no matter what's going on in your life and regardless of the noise buzzing around the Internet, you have a framework from which to move forward and create your business with integrity, based in your inner world, on what you have to give and share, not on your want and need to make money. That is how truly successful people become successful, they tap into who they are and what they love and build their lives and businesses around that.

Creating your business from the place of your unique vision and mission is critical. You need to have your own thing to focus on. If you don't you're probably wasting a lot of time and perhaps money following disingenuous marketers who know how to market the perception of value in products and services but hold no *real* value for you. Having your own thing allows you to say no, when the advertisements and emails start popping up telling you, you have to opt in for this or that. Protect yourself from information overload. Stay focused on what you're doing.

If you're feeling some resistance to clarifying your vision, purpose or mission, remember that where you are is how you feel, and it's ok. There is no need to rush through the process. Try holding the intention that your *soul's purpose* is being revealed to you. Just ask it to come and stay alert. It will reveal itself. Trust that you know. But do not prolong the process either. Write something down. It can always be adjusted later. Not everything that you think is part of your vision now will pan out or be part of your vision later. Just start and be open to course correction as you move forward.

Here's how my Soul's Purpose and business mission statements are shaping up.

My Soul's Purpose is to use my gift of communication to empower people to live purpose-filled free lives.

or

My Soul's Purpose is to use my love of having a good conversation to inspire and empower people to live on purpose and in total freedom.

From my Soul's Purpose I'm developing my businesses mission statement.

Our (my) mission is to empower people all around the world to live and work on their own terms. Based in these four principles of personal growth; learning, giving, taking action and feeling good, we (I) create, sell and are affiliated with products and services that focus on creating "success" from the inside out.

Through our workshops, seminars and speaking events we assist individuals in the positive transformation of their lives and businesses as we support them on their journey as enlightened human beings.

The world's most famous mission statement

While doing research on mission statements, I came across several references that pointed to the US Declaration Of Independence as being a prime example of a well crafted mission. I'm inclined to agree... how about you?

"We hold these truths to be self-evident, that all men are created equal, that they are endowed by their Creator with certain unalienable Rights, that among these are Life, Liberty, and the pursuit of Happiness. That to secure these rights, Governments are instituted among Men, deriving their just powers from the consent of the governed. That whenever any Form of Government becomes destructive of these ends, it is the Right of the People to alter or to abolish it, and to institute new Government, laying its foundation on such principles and organizing its powers in such form, as to them shall seem most likely to effect their Safety and Happiness."

More examples of mission statements

Facebook: *"Facebook's mission is to give people the power to share and make the world more open and connected."*

Google: *"To organize the world's information and make it universally accessible and useful."*

Disney: *"We create happiness by providing the finest in entertainment for people of all ages, everywhere."*

Apple: *"Apple designs Macs, the best personal computers in the world."*

FRAMING YOUR GREAT CONVERSATION: INNER WORK & ACTION STEPS

INNER WORK

Find a quiet place. Sit quietly and bring your attention to the energy point above your head. Feel the connecting energy between that point and your heart center. With your focus there, ask, *what do I have to give?* Observe what comes up. When you are ready, write your insights down in your notebook.

Keep in mind that your insights may show up as images, words, sounds or feelings. Whatever they are, write them down, even if they don't make any sense to you right now.

OUTER WORK ACTION STEPS

Write your Personal Statement of Purpose.
Write your Soul's Purpose statement.
Write your Business Mission statement.

GO A LITTLE FURTHER

Read the article, The Having Space (included in the Resource section).

Any questions? Email me at gemeem@makelifeworknow.com.

My Personal Statement of Purpose

_____

_____

_____

_____

_____

_____

_____

_____

_____

_____

_____

_____

_____

_____

_____

_____

My Soul's Purpose

_____

_____

_____

_____

_____

_____

_____

My Businesses Mission Statement

_____

_____

_____

_____

_____

_____

_____

FOCUS YOUR GREAT CONVERSATION

Congratulations, what you've done by articulating your soul's purpose and business mission is set the parameters in which *You* want to live and work. I believe this is the most liberating thing you can do for yourself. By having a soul/business mission in place you are now in agreement with your higher self. You have decided to no longer live and work by default. You've set your own direction.

In the space between the awareness of your current situation and the fulfillment of your purpose is the opportunity to focus your attention, energy and resources. In this third step in the Make Life Work program you will do that by creating goals. But not just any goals. Your goals will be infused with *achievability*. The key to that is to align your goals with your purpose or at the very least have a compelling reason for pursuing them.

Without grounding your goals in purpose, in meaning, you're liable to fall into the perpetual "goal setting" trap. You know, where you set goal after goal, year after year and never end up actually achieving what you want. Don't feel bad if this has been your experience. This type of compulsive behavior, of doing things over and over again seems to be engrained in our cultural psyche. In fact, entire industry's thrive on it. I'm thinking... the diet and exercise industry. You know, most of them don't actually want you to lose the weight. They want you to keep setting the goal to *try* to lose weight so they can keep you as a paying customer.

The processes offered here in <u>Make Life Work</u> are intended to assist you in taking your goal setting out of an exercise in wishful thinking, where you think you want something but have no real intention to have it, into the development of a skill you can use to achieve or manifest the things and experiences that resonate with *You*.

When you set a goal, what you're actually doing is creating an opportunity for yourself to move in the direction of your passion/ purpose/mission. Goals are *you*, taking ownership of the creative process. It's you sending a message back to your higher self saying yes, I'm ready to take on the responsibility of having (whatever your goal is) this in my life...now.

On the following pages you will learn how to create goals that are B.I.G. and S.M.A.R.T.!

IF YOUR GOALS ARE NOT B.I.G. THEY'RE NOT WORTH PURSUING

Often when we think about setting goals, we think about them in relation to time. The tendency is to set long (5 to 10 yrs.), medium (3 to 5yrs.) and short term (6 months to 3yrs.) goals. Well, I don't know about you but for me that approach just has not worked.

Having long term goals is not necessary. You already have a purpose and/or mission. That's really all you need to manifest your desires into the world. Attaching a date to them that's way off into the future is counter productive. My personal belief is that having long terms goals is nothing more than unconscious programming that keeps you separated from enjoying life in the present moment. Replace your belief in the necessity of setting long terms goals with a commitment to fully live NOW.

Goals keep you focused on your purpose and mission. Think of them as specific actions you take NOW that will allow your vision to unfold the way you want it to.

When I sit down to write out my goals, my first thought is not on when I will have it completed. That's too much pressure for me. The first thing I do with a goal is put it through the B.I.G. test. That is, are my goals *bold*? What is the *intention* behind it and is it an expression of *gratitude?*

Bold

To be bold is to be courageous and daring. When you think about your goals being bold consider the following:

•Does this goal stretch you outside of your comfort zone or are you playing it safe?
•Will you gain more confidence as a result of pursuing it?
•If your goal was an announcement and/or reflection of the greatest part of you, what is it saying about you?

Intention

When you create goals that have intention, what you're essentially doing is assigning meaning to it and making a commitment to act in a certain way. The question you want to ask yourself when you are contemplating your intention is, why? Why am I doing what I'm doing? What do I want to see and experience for myself and others as a result of pursuing this goal?

Gratitude

Oftentimes when people engage the goal setting process, it becomes a rote routine in writing down the things they want. All the while clinging to the notion that happiness awaits them once the goal is completed, in the future. Well, life doesn't happen in the future. It happens now. When putting your goals through the B.I.G. test, get in touch with what it is about the goal that elicits the most gratitude in you and start feeling it NOW. If you can get yourself to feeling grateful in the present moment for whatever it is you're pursuing, you know you are on the right track.

Be certain your goals pass the B.I.G. test. Once they have, you can consider the time element when you make them S.M.A.R.T.

S.M.A.R.T. GOALS PROVIDE THE FRAMEWORK FOR MAKING YOUR GOALS WORKABLE

After your goals have passed the B.I.G. test you can use the popular goal setting practice of converting them into S.M.A.R.T. goals. Below is a breakdown of what the S.M.A.R.T. acronym means.

Specific

To be specific is to be free and clear from ambiguity. A goal that is specific answers the who, what, when, where and why questions.

Measurable

Build steps into your goals that mark your progress as you move toward achievement. To measure progress in your goals you answer questions like, how much, how many and by when.

Attainable

This is all about belief. You must believe that your goals are do-able NOW, and that the successful achievement of your goals is not the result of a condition you will meet in the future. You can attain just about any goal you set if you believe you are worthy of having it and are willing and capable of doing what it takes to achieve it.

Relevant

Your goals must relate to something. It must be rooted in something that holds meaning for you. An easy way to ensure that your goals are relevant is to make certain that in some way, shape or form, they relate to your vision, purpose and/or business mission.

Timely

It is important that you have a time frame to work within. Otherwise, you will always find ways to justify why your goals can't be achieved *now*. If you want to sell 5,000 e-books on the internet, when do you want to do that?

*I suggest ditching long term goals all together and focusing on the NOW. When setting a time frame for you goals make it as short as possible... less than a year sounds good.

One more thing about goals

Although it's a good practice to write goals in a S.M.A.R.T. way, it's important that you stay open. You really don't have to know exactly *how* you will manifest them. Your job is only to communicate what you want to the Universe clearly and to trust that whatever your asking for is already here. This, by the way is why the G in the B.I.G. goals criteria is so important. Gratitude is a powerful emotion. As much as humanly possible, you want to feel the feelings of having what you want now. When you are feeling you are sending a powerful message to *You*, The Universe, God, that is evidence of your belief and trust that *it* is already done. Expressing gratitude is a life and business best practice.

Examples of B.I.G. S.M.A.R.T Goals

B.I.G. Goal

The <u>Make Life Work Personal Growth Program</u> is a global organization!

Written S.M.A.R.T.

I will produce and lead three successful <u>Make Life Work</u> live workshops by February 1, 2012. I will create a power-point presentation by June 30, 2011 and secure the venue, date, and time for the first live event by July 30, 2011.

B.I.G. Goal

I have an email list of 10,000 people or more!

Written S.M.A.R.T.

I am committed to building a targeted email list of 10,000 people interested in personal growth and creating a sustainable online business by December 1, 2011. I have created valuable content that serves the needs of my list by April 30, 2011. This content includes written reports, audio, video and email marketing. I attract powerful win/win JV partnerships with top personal growth experts and online marketers to help me in this effort.

FOCUS YOUR GREAT CONVERSATION: INNER WORK & ACTION STEPS

INNER WORK

Find a quiet place. Sit quietly and bring your attention to the energy point above your head. From that point focus your attention on your purpose/mission. Feel the connection, the energy flowing between your energy point and your heart. Now, *consciously ask* for guidance and/or the next steps you need to take to manifest your Soul's Purpose and your B.I.G. S.M.A.R.T. Goals.

OUTER WORK ACTION STEPS

Immediately following your inner work exercise in consciously asking, create a *Possibilities List*. Your Possibilities List is a list of things you can do to fulfill your purpose. Ultimately it is a list of things that excite you! Write down any and everything, even if it seems crazy impossible!

Choose one to three things from your Possibilities List and put them through the B.I.G. test.

Once your goals have passed the B.I.G. test, convert them into S.M.A.R.T. goals.

GO A LITTLE FURTHER

Go back and look over your assessment statements. If you have found that you are not where you want to be in any area of your life, make a commitment now to change that. Create a goal that represents where you want to be. Put it through the B.I.G. test, then write it in a S.M.A.R.T. way.

Create a Vision Board.

A great way to help you FOCUS is to use images. Having a vision board is a wonderful way to help you manifest what you want faster. I've learned a simple way to really energize my board from Marie Diamond. See the Personal Growth Powerhouses section for more information.

Any questions? Email me at gemeem@makelifeworknow.com.

My Possibilities List

My B.I.G. Goals

Goal #1

_____

_____

_____

_____

_____

Goal #2

_____

_____

_____

_____

Goal #3

_____

_____

_____

_____

My B.I.G. Goals re-written in a S.M.A.R.T. Way

Goal #1

_____

_____

_____

_____

_____

Goal #2

_____

_____

_____

_____

Goal #3

_____

_____

_____

_____

_____

MASTER YOUR GREAT CONVERSATION

Yes! You're in the home stretch. Let's review.

So now you know that you are more than you physical body and the language *You* (the within you) use to communicate with you (the physical you) are your thoughts, feelings and emotions. This communication is *Your Great Conversation* and everything that shows up in your life, your health, your money, your relationships and your business are the results of this all encompassing conversation.

You've started practicing the "inner work" of being conscious of Your Great Conversation by focusing on the expanded version of you, paying particular attention to your spiritual body and the energy point above your head. Your "outer work" has taken you through an assessment of the *7 Key Indicators of Where You Are* and tracking exercises to give you a good honest look at your current circumstances, allowing you to SEE where you are.

You got clear on *what you have to give* by articulating your soul's purpose and/or business mission and committed to sharing what you have by creating B.I.G. S.M.A.R.T. goals, essentially DRAWING where *You* want to be.

In this final section of <u>Make Life Work</u>, we're going to turn our attention to what you can do to manifest your vision and create your successful business more quickly and easily. Note, we are not going to focus on "how" to do this with a laundry list of things like setting up a web site, choosing the best auto-responder or developing a marketing strategy. Getting a handle on those things are quite necessary if you want to thrive as a solo entrepreneur, however if you try to rush and do them without knowing that you have to become, the *Master of Your Great Conversation*, your efforts in that direction will be wasted.

In a strategic plan the "think" stage of the process focuses on what specific actions need to be taken in order to close the gap between a company's current situation and their ideal vision and mission. In *Mastering Your Conversation*, our purpose is the same.

To close the gap between where you are and where you want to be, you have to know what's in the gap. Do you know what's in your gap? The answer is the same for everybody who feels stuck or *never* seems to achieve what they set out to do, have or be. If you've heard it once, you've probably heard it a thousand times. But seriously, the only *things* between where you are and where you want to be are old patterns of beliefs and behavior, commonly referred to as your habits, programming or mindset. That, in addition to the *feelings* these things elicit in you are the only things standing in the way of your success. In *Mastering Your Conversation*, we're going to work on how to transform the *stuff* that's in your gap by developing habits, both thought and behavioral that support what you *really* want... freedom, abundance, happiness, and joy, right?

You should know before you start the process of your mastery that none of the suggestions I make are mandatory. It is possible to have a spontaneous breakthrough. You can release the stuff clouding you up by simply relaxing into the intention to release it and move forward. I practice both. I do what I suggest and I release through meditation on the continuous flow of well being and light pouring into me at all times as well as the love, power, forgiveness and detachment that is in me, around me and coming through me. In any case, only do what feels right for you.

GETTING TO YOUR "ALLOWING" IS WHAT MASTERY IS ALL ABOUT

To allow is to let something Be... with ease.

Let's be clear, *The Great Conversation* is ongoing. It does not stop. For as long as you're breathing (and perhaps beyond that) and have thoughts and feelings, you are in it. Since this is the case you might as well make it, better yet, *allow* it to *work* for you.

It may be helpful to think of *The Great Conversation* as an exchange of creative energy between the unknown aspects of *You* and the physical you. Your objective is to get in and stay in the flow of this energy so you can allow your desires to manifest in the world.

Staying in the flow has proven to be challenging for many people, especially entrepreneurs seeking success on the internet. If this is you, it's important to know that your lack of flow, which translates to a lack of success is not because your business isn't meant to be, it's because at some level you are in conflict. You may be screaming intellectually, "YES! I want to have, be or do x, y and z" but on a feeling or emotional level you may have an abundance of doubt and fear that's uncertain and sending mixed messages to your higher self about what you want to have, be or do. Settling this inner conflict is the practice of your mastery and how you begin *allowing*.

A simple shift in your awareness can open up your allowing.

There's a predominant belief in the world that says when we want something, be it a car, house, business, book or a cup of coffee we have to go out and get it. We accept that *things* in the physical world exists outside and separate from us. This couldn't be further from the truth. Science has long since proved that everything in our universe is made up of the same thing. Energy. You are energy, money is energy, your business is energy.

Energy exists. It cannot be created or destroyed, just transformed. Therefore, any and everything that you want *already exists*. Instead of believing you have to "go get" what you want, *practice* accepting the belief that you already have everything. My personal belief is that once you say you want something, it is instantaneously created and resides in your personal energy field. I sometimes call this field, my *Having Space*, it's also referred to as the Universe, The Vortex, Heaven, the place of *All That Is*. All you have to do is believe that what you want is there and call it down into the physical realm.

Believing that your desires, including your successful business is already here is a major paradigm shift in the traditional "how to create a business" process. Most people don't believe at all. They just start working and wonder if or when a successful business will show up.

Allow your business to *Be*, first.

SETTLING INNER CONFLICT

It's all about communicating a consistent vibration so that what you want resonates with you.

I'm going to take a leap of faith now and assume that if you're reading this book, you've heard the phrase, "thoughts become things". That's an abbreviated version of *"your thoughts determine your feelings, your feelings determine your actions and your actions determine your results."* You may have also heard, "form follows thought". In any case, what each of those phrases point to is the fact that your thoughts play a key role in what shows up in your life.

Ever since the hugely successful movie, The Secret made its debut in 2006, the *law of attraction* has received a lot of attention in the self help and make money online industries. Its release marks the first time in history that the knowledge of the law of attraction was made accessible to the masses on such a large scale. The law of attraction states the universal principle of *like attracts like*. Which simply means that what you focus on, you will attract. The stronger the focus, the more expansive the *essence* of the thing your focused on will become.

When it comes to creating your business, *like attracts like* does not mean that you have to have *(on a physical level)* a successful business in order to *attract* a successful business. It means you have to offer a vibration that resonates with success. You simply cannot *feel* like a unsuccessful failure and expect to *attract* a successful business. Your feelings are the language of life. What you consistently feel *is* what your communicating to *You*, no matter what words come out of your mouth. You must be clear, certain, aligned, in your communication with *You* in order to deliberately and consciously create the life and business you want.

If you're dealing with inner conflict (and you know you are if you've been trying or wanting something for a long time), it's incumbent on you to settle it. Doing so, strengthens your point of attraction, allowing what you want to recognize you - to vibe with you - to move at your same speed - to resonate with and flow to you. Your *successful* life and business depends on it.

You can work with your day to day choices and activities and the power of your mind to settle inner conflict and strengthen your point of attraction. On the following pages you will find ways to work with both.

DO YOU KNOW WHERE YOU'RE COMING FROM?

Are you "set" on abundance and success or lack and failure?

Fulfilling your purpose and achieving your goals has less to do with your level of skill and more to do with your positioning and habits. Your positioning, *where you're coming from,* is not the physical place in which you live or your status in any given industry. It's where you're coming from *energetically*. It's your point of attraction or "set" point.

Many entrepreneurs are set on lack and failure without being conscious of it. They start business after business yielding little to no positive results, wondering why. This is because somewhere along the line, and it doesn't matter where, they entertained and consumed the idea of lack. If this is you don't worry. Your mind, being the dutiful servant it is, did what it was supposed to do. It created programs, a blueprint in your energy field, *habits,* that supported your belief. This is not right or wrong, good or bad. It's just that now that you're trying your hand at success, your intellectual mind and subconscious mind are in conflict. But, there is good news. If you're set on lack and failure, you can change it!

You can replace your old programming with new ones. To do that you must first recognize the need to do so. That's what *Exploring The Language of Life* and the self assessment was all about. It was you becoming *aware*. Once you are aware and accept what is, offering no resistance to it, you can begin consciously re-programming and repositioning yourself.

Acting As If is a great way to start

Please note, I'm not advocating the concept of "faking it until you make it". In my experience, faking it lends itself to the justification of lying to yourself and others, which is counter-productive. If you're faking it, the people around you and your potential customers will be able to feel the BS a mile away and will not trust you. But what's worse, you will not believe and trust in yourself. In your mastery, *acting as if* is the conscious practice of abundance. It is recognizing you already have more than you think, trusting in that *having* and *acting* upon it in the NOW.

Acting As If will help you develop both the mindset and habits that support you consciously coming from a place of abundance and success.

Below are three easy ways I've chosen to *act as if*. You can choose to integrate all three ideas simultaneously or you can take them on one by one. In any case, practice, practice, practice and you will begin to see changes in your life immediately.

#1: Become an Investor

Generally speaking, an investor is someone who uses money to buy or participate in a business venture with the expectation of a future profit, otherwise known as a favorable return on investment or ROI.

In other words, an investor is willing to pay the price NOW for what they *expect* to return to them in the future. As you move forward with creating your ideal life and business, ask yourself, what are the costs involved and are you willing to pay the price NOW for your future benefit?

And yes, there is always a price. The price for achieving your objectives, especially the ones associated with creating your business will undoubtedly include payments of time, intellectual and creative thought, material and monetary resources. The buy-in involves risks and consequences that must be evaluated. If you are willing to pay the price, congratulations, keep going, there is nothing to stop you from achieving your goals. If you are unsure, stop immediately and re-evaluate.

How to practice being an Investor: Investors spend money to acquire assets. You are your greatest asset, so spend money on yourself. As a practical matter, consider setting aside a specific percentage of your income, be it weekly, bi-weekly or monthly in an account other than the one you use for paying bills. Keep the money in the account and do not take it out for any reason other than to invest in gaining knowledge and new skills associated with your most important business goals and personal growth.

Investing in my personal growth is one of the best decisions I've ever made. My latest investment took me to Minnesota, to a Learning Strategies retreat. As a result, my life has transformed. I gained more knowledge and the energy boost I needed to complete writing this book. I also made some important new business contacts and life long friends. The money it cost to attend that workshop is nothing compared to what I got in return. Take the leap. Invest in yourself.

#2: Get outside yourself and become a Giver

As an investor you expect a return. You expect to receive. As a *Giver* you have no expectations (except perhaps warm and fuzzy feelings). To move forward in your life in a balanced way, it is wise to cultivate both the receiver and giver in you. Giving is good for the mind and the spirit. It takes the pressure off obsessive thinking about you and your goals and focuses your attention on a purpose greater than yourself.

Giving is an expression of freedom. When you operate from a giving mindset, you have options. As a giver you exercise your ability to make choices and base your actions on your own internal values and beliefs. People who do not operate with a giving mindset and heart often feel restricted or limited and withhold their resources, denying themselves the freedom to live life on their own terms. They do things they think they have to do. Doing things out of obligation (real or imagined) is like being in jail where there is no choice and people do what they are told 24/7. Free people do what they want because they can. You were born free. Exercise your freedom.

How to practice being a Giver: Stop withholding and give. If you have money to pay bills, you have money to give to a worthy cause. Take some time to think about issues you care about. Research and make a list of organizations that are doing good work in this area and commit to a making a monetary gift. Your gift does not have to be large, just consistent. You want your giving to become an effortless habit, so make the payment as automatic as paying your bills. Have it come directly out of your paycheck or bank account. It is not necessary to get anyone's permission or tell anyone what you are doing. If you are excited about a cause or a particular organization you can share details about the organization without disclosing what your gift is.

In addition to giving money, there are probably a billion different ways you can discipline yourself to be a Giver. You can volunteer your time and/or other resources like food and clothing to a charitable organization, you can be a mentor or provide professional services in your particular area of expertise. You can practice giving a smile to strangers. Everyone has something to contribute. Choose one and do that. But by all means, do not over commit! Over-committing is counter-productive and will only make you feel bad for not sticking to your word (I know this from experience). You want to *feel good* about what you are doing, not add unnecessary pressure and stress to your life.

My personal favorite giving practice is to be a mentor. I've mentored women transitioning from prison back into society. A little girl with HIV. A girl in high school getting ready to go to college. An intern who worked with me. I've spent Saturdays with elementary school kids, talking, taking photos and just having fun. Mentoring is my way. What's yours?

#3: Open up to the possibility of more, right here, right now

When people are unhappy they tend to "need change". That needing is often just an excuse to cut and run, so they can look for happiness some place else. The problem with that is, *you always show up wherever you go*. So no matter where you are, you repeat the same types of experiences over and over again just with different players. Get off this merry-go-round. Break the habit of needing change by opening up to more, right here, right now. You can do that by focusing your attention on things that will improve the situation you are currently in instead of leaving it. I like to think of it as *maxing out* all your possibilities.

How to practice opening up to more *(if you're an entrepreneur who still has a job)*: So many people go to work every day and loose out. They let free money, good resources and access to knowledge (education) slip right through their fingers because they either do not know or have failed to take advantage of the benefits available to them. As a practical exercise and before you make another move, check with your human resources department to be sure you are taking advantage of *all* company benefits, retirement and tax savings, health care, continued education, etc. When you are finished asking and signing up for those things, ask, *what else?*

Taking advantage of everything that's being offered to you through your employer is not the only way you can open up at your job. Considered offering *what you have to give* to them, even if it doesn't fit into your current job description. You never know what opportunities await you.

If you are a full time online entrepreneur, you may also be letting opportunities slip through your fingers. Are you wasting your time and money on programs and services you don't use. Who are you paying to do what? Are you taking full advantage of their services? Who are you partnering with? Are you in a win/win situation with them? Everybody's so focused on social networking and the power of sites like Facebook and Twitter. How are you utilizing those sites? Have you reached out to any of your like minded "friends" to network and/or collaborate with? Take stock of your business. If you can't find a way to *max out* your current circumstances and business relationships, let them go. It's ok...really.

The decision to start my business came directly out of my sincere desire to open up to the possibilities of where I was. And, where I was, was at a job I did not want to be in. Then, one day, the onsite professional development trainer said, "we don't expect that you all will be here forever, but we do expect that you give us your best." For the rest of the day I contemplated what was my best. When the day was over, I had made the decision that I wasn't going to run away from my unwanted job situation. I was going to offer them the very best of me. Whether they accepted it or not was not my concern. A few months later, the professional development director got a proposal from me titled, Make Work, Work: Strategic Planning For Every Employee. The core ideas presented in that draft compelled me to start my training and consulting business and have also made its way into this book, Make Life Work: Personal Growth For Today's Entrepreneur. Not bad, huh!

So there you have it. Three ways you can begin your practice of *acting as if.* Doing so will help you change *where you're coming from,* and "set" your mind, your point of attraction, firmly on abundance.

WORKING WITH AFFIRMATIONS

Words are powerful.

Words are the bridge between what you think and what you do. Choose them wisely and they will accelerate your "having". Choose them poorly and they'll reek havoc in your life and keep you separated from what you want. In your mastery, you can use words to soften or relax inner conflict so that your vibe is one, at peace, and resonating with what you want.

An affirmation is a declaration of something that is true. It really doesn't matter what you are affirming. If you say it often enough, you'll begin to feel the power of your statement, your subconscious mind will then accept it as truth and you will develop habits that support your belief then behave accordingly. Use affirmations to create your own truth and train yourself into agreement with that.

When writing affirmations keep the following in mind:

Write them in the present tense

You want what you want in the here and now. If you write and then say affirmations that say something like, "one day I will have" or "I'm always within arm's reach of my goals", you'll never get what you want. What you are asking for will always be one day away or at an arms reach from you.

Be positive

Focus on what you want, *not* on what you don't want. For example if your affirmation is, *I'm loosing weight.* The focus of that statement is on loss. Stating what you want that way sends mixed message to your higher self. You don't really want to loose do you? Instead affirm the end result you are seeking, *I am slim and trim or I'm enjoying my slim and physically fit body!*

Keep it brief

You want your affirmations to be fun and easy to remember. It may be helpful to think about your affirmations as little snapshots of your goals. It's like, "click" that's it.

Use I am statements and actions words

I am...enjoying, loving, empowering, sharing, revealing...

Say or read them as much as possible

Say them in the morning, afternoon and/or evening. Hang them on your vision board, keep them in your notebook, post them on Facebook. Do whatever feels good to you. Just work with them everyday. I find myself automatically saying "everything's working out for me" throughout my day. And guess what, everything I'm engaged in is working out for me. There's amazing power in keeping your affirmations out where you can see them. It will compel you to say them either out loud or silently more frequently.

Sample Affirmations

- Everything's working out for me!
- I exceed *all* expectations.
- I create value in my client's lives!
- I am a leader with integrity!
- I am whole, perfect, strong, powerful, loving, harmonious and happy. *~ Joseph Murphy, from The Power of Your Subconscious Mind*
- Yes We Can!
- I've got the power!
- I am so happy and grateful NOW. Money flows to me in increasing quantities, through multiple sources, on a continuous basis. *~Bob Proctor*
- I am joyfully crossing the finish line of the New York City Marathon!
- I am a NY Times Best Selling Author!
- I am a generous giver and excellent receiver. *~T. Harv Eker*
- Money comes frequently and easily.

Here's an affirmation that I say every morning now - it is based on my Soul's Purpose & business mission

I, Gemeem Davis, here and now, am empowering people all around the world to live enlighted, purpose-filled, free lives.

Here's an affirmation one of my FB friends posted on his wall.

I am Mr. Excellence. I am a walking reflection of success and happiness. I improve myself in some way, every day of my life. I read, I listen, I learn and I win! ~ John Ramsey

MASTER YOUR CONVERSATION: INNER WORK & ACTION STEPS

INNER WORK

Find a quiet place. Sit quietly, close your eyes and bring your attention to the energy point above your head. Feel the connection between that point and your heart center. You don't have to ask for anything. Everything you've ever wanted has already been created, including your ultra successful business. Trust this the case. See your business in your minds eye and surround it in golden light. Bring this business down into the here and now. Feel it pass through all the levels of *You*, feel it touch your spirit, your point of attraction. Allow it to enter your heart center. Hold it there for a moment then release it. Know, that it is done. Say, thank you! When you're ready, open your eyes and journal what you experienced.

OUTER WORK ACTION STEPS

Start "acting as if." Become an *Investor, Giver and Open Up*. I recommend integrating all three approaches into your life as soon as possible, but it is okay to commit to one habit building action at a time. The speed in which you progress will blow your mind!

Have FUN with affirmations. You can create an affirmation for each of the *7 Key Indicators of Where You Are*, your purpose, business mission and your goals. Create however many you like, for whatever it is you want to see and experience in your life. Write them, say them, record them, make them your screen saver, put them on your vision board, your refrigerator, and/or post them on your social media pages. Whatever you do, repeat them as much as possible throughout your day for however long it takes. Write at least one affirmation for each of your B.I.G. S.M.A.R.T. goals.

GO A LITTLE FURTHER

Feel Gratitude. Expressing your gratitude is a life and business *best practice*. Keep a journal, speak it out loud with your partner or simply close your eyes at the end of the night and offer a silent, *thank you*. Any way you choose is fine... just do it!

Any questions? Email me at gemeem@makelifeworknow.com.

My Affirmations

Soul's Purpose Affirmations

_____

_____

_____

_____

_____

_____

_____

Businesses Mission Affirmations

_____

_____

_____

_____

_____

_____

_____

7 Key Affirmations

YOU'VE ONLY JUST BEGUN

Personal growth is a practice. Personal growth is a practice. Personal growth is a practice. Got it? Good :-) That is why <u>Make Life Work</u> is a *work*-book and not just a book for you to read. Integrating what you learn into your daily life is how you will grow a richer, happier, more fulfilling life and have the business and lifestyle you desire.

By completing the <u>Make Life Work</u> program, you now have four very important and powerful documents, your <u>Personal Statement of Purpose</u>, that outlined your vision for your life and business, your <u>Soul's Purpose</u> and <u>Business Mission Statement</u>, your <u>B.I.G. S.M.A.R.T. Goals</u> and your <u>Affirmations</u>. These are your freedom papers, your <u>Personal Declaration of Independence</u>. Keep them visible and refer to them on a daily basis.

Every second, of every minute, of every hour, of every day, you are in constant communication with *You*. Your conscious awareness of this conversation, *Your Great Conversation* is how you navigate your way through life. Your feelings are the *Language of You*. This is the same for everybody, so rest assured you are on a level playing field.

Your thinking mind is a tool. It is not the place from which you create. You do that with your spirit and you get confirmation of that creation in your *feeling body*, which incidentally has a mind of its own. It is your heart.

It's imperative to your success that you understand and practice creating from the spirit and the heart, from the inside, on a continuous basis. Your thinking mind can then be relied upon to do what it does best, help you execute your heart felt desires by developing programs and habits that support *You*. I say this not to suggest that you totally negate your mind. Everything has its purpose and it is true that the mind plays a major role in what you experience. But you do have to relax it.

The work you've done here has given you a solid foundation from which you can build the life and business you want. Your job now is to trust what you've put together. If you trust, you will not worry about what others are doing and you'll be shielded from "information overload". So, trust and stay consciously connected to *You*. All the right, next steps to build the life and business you've been dreaming about will become clear. Watch for them.

You are now at your new beginning... Ready?

PRACTICAL TIPS FOR NEW ONLINE ENTREPRENEURS OR ANYBODY MARKETING STUFF ON THE INTERNET!

The following tips are for people who are brand spanking new to starting an online or home based business. I feel confident in offering you these few tips on the practical aspects of starting your business not because I am an expert Internet marketer, but because when I made my debut online I made a lot of mistakes which resulted in an abundance of wasted time, money and energy. Here's to my failing forward, so hopefully you won't have to.

Tip #1

Do the "inner work" and "outer action steps" suggested throughout <u>Make Life Work</u>. I trust I've made a compelling argument to do so in the pages you've just finished reading. If you do, your niche or target market will be made abundantly clear to you.

Tip #2

Don't fool yourself or let anybody convince you that it's ok to skip the steps of success. Clarity, choice and action is the only way. If someone wants you to forgo any part of the process, they probably don't have your best interest at heart. You've got to do the work. Your business is a reflection of what's going on inside of you. Period.

Tip #3

Get a coach, mentor, or consultant. Starting any business, whether online or off can sometimes feel like a daunting task. Trust me, you need support. And if you can find someone to show you the ropes and help keep your spirits up in the process, you'll move along a lot faster.

Tip #4

Opt out of all those lists! You know you're not going to buy anything from most of them. They're just clogging up your email box and your flow.

Tip #5

As an online entrepreneur, your #1 business goal is to build a email list of targeted prospects. You can do that through a website or blog by offering visitors "free" information in exchange for signing up to your email list. (I have a website and use AWeber.com to capture leads and do email marketing).

Tip #6

Talk about what you do to anyone who will listen. Be confident and enthusiastic. You never know what connections can be made. (I totally blew this one a few times… I actually talked someone out of hiring me to speak at their company because I was playing small).

Tip #7

Create your own product(s). That's if you want to be a leader in your market.

Tip #8

Monetize your business by becoming an affiliate. But only promote products and programs that you have personally used and believe in.

Stay in your integrity! Check out my Online Resources. I am an affiliate for some of them).

Tip #9

After you finish the Make Life Work program, it would be wise to invest in a program offered by one or two of the Internet marketing "gurus" to help you focus on how to create and sell content on the Internet. (I wish I would have done this from the get go…regrets regrets…but I learned a lot :-)

Tip #10

Be consistent with your communication to your list. That means, have an email marketing strategy. That doesn't mean you have to bombard people five times per week with emails and newsletters but if you say you're going to do something do it. Remember, you are building a relationship with real people. (I actually wasted a lot of money not being consistent. I was paying Constant Contact about $25 bucks a month and not sending out any communication. That may not sound like a lot but it adds up…quickly. Never mind what it cost me in reputation to my clients and potentials).

Tip #11

Observe what successful people in your industry are doing. You can even model their business strategy but bring your authentic self to that model. After receiving several cookie-cutter marketing messages people tend to become jaded and feel exploited. You certainly don't want your customers to feel like that when they receive your offer.

Tip #12

Look for ways you can support others in achieving their goals. Form partnerships that promote a win-win-win-win atmosphere. That's a win for you, your partner, your clients and humanity as a whole.

Tip #13

Read <u>Crush It! Why Now Is The Time To Cash In On Your Passion</u> by Gary Vaynerchuk. Gary will teach you about the importance of developing a personal brand then walk you step by step through the process of creating yours on the Internet. This is a must have book if you are serious about building an online business... and I don't say that lightly. He's the one to watch... and model. Check it at www.crushitbook.com.

Also read <u>The 4-Hour Workweek</u> by Timothy Ferris. This is an excellent book that gives you everything, and I mean everything you need to take real world action to design and live the NR (New Rich) lifestyle. Buy the book and check out his website and blog at www.fourhourworkweek.com.

Tip #14

Release, release, release! Release all doubts, fears, expectations, needs, any and everything associated with you identifying with, and having a successful business. Practice being open (just breathe with it) to all opportunities presenting themselves to you. Stay focused and present in the NOW. You'll either have a successful online business or something even better will come along!

ONLINE RESOURCES

There are probably hundreds if not thousands of inexpensive online resources available to help you build your Internet presence. The following are the few that I use and are perfect for newbies just getting their feet wet on the Internet.

Setting up a basic website

When I put together my first website, I had no idea what I was doing, so consequently I made mistakes. Mistake #1, I registered my domain name and got web hosting from Yahoo.com. Don't get me wrong, their service is easy enough to use (especially if you have a PC) and their customer service is awesome but they are more expensive compared to other services and because I have a Mac and not a PC, I was severely restricted in what I could do with their templates... I couldn't even place widgets on my website.

Now I use GoDaddy, https://www.godaddy.com to register domain names, host my website and get web based email addresses. To design the site, I use a simple template in iWeb that I can easily manipulate and publish to GoDaddy.com.

Lots of online entrepreneurs and marketers use the free WordPress software to create their websites and blogs. At http://wordpress.org you can publish a blog for free. With the free account your blog address will be yourname.wordpress.com or you can opt to pay $17.00 bucks a year to get a customized address without wordpress in the URL. They have great FREE templates they call Themes for you to use to design your blog, which actually functions like a website. If

I had done a little research before I jumped on the Internet to set up a website, I probably would have opted to use WordPress first. What can I say, when you know better, you do better.

Email Marketing/List Management

If you read Tip # 5, you know the most important goal for your online business is to build an email list. To do that you will need a Opt-in form to place on your website and create a series of auto-responder messages to build a relationship with your list. This is Email Marketing 101. I first used <u>Constant Contact</u> for my email marketing solutions because they have really good professional looking newsletter templates that are easy to use. But their auto-responder capabilities are very limited, so I switched to <u>AWeber.com.</u> It's inexpensive and the basic service for a small list (under 500 subscribers) is only $19.00 a month plus it's very easy to use. I highly recommend it. <u>Sign Up for just $1.00</u>

Note:

There are lots of other email marketing/list management services you might want to consider. Base your decision on the current needs and size of your email list. You can always upgrade as your list gets bigger and your company grows. Do your research and check out, <u>iContact</u>, <u>GetResponse</u>, <u>1ShoppingCart</u> and <u>InfusionSoft</u> among others.

Video Marketing

Video's are a great way to create content for you website or blog. You can share them on a FREE platform like <u>YouTube</u> to drive traffic to your website. These video's do not need to be high budget major productions, just simple two to five minute video's you can make with your webcam or video camera. For more creative video making I found a great resource in <u>Animoto</u>. I started out using the FREE version but quickly upgraded to the $30.00 a year *All Access* version. It's so worth it and the videos are easy and fun to make!

Article Marketing

A great way to generate traffic to your website or blog and build "Expert" status in your niche is to write articles and post them for FREE on websites like <u>SelfGrowth.com</u>, <u>EzineArticles.com</u> and <u>Articlesnatch</u>. There are tons of sites out there. Just google "article marketing" and you'll see. At SelfGrowth.com you can set up an "expert" profile and link your articles directly to your page. You can also provide a link to your website or blog right on your expert profile page. Additionally, you can connect with thousands of other experts in your field. Check out my expert profile at <u>http://www.selfgrowth.com/experts/gemeem_davis</u> and consider setting up a page for yourself.

Social Media

You just have to get yourself out there. You'll never sell anything online if you don't get people to know, like and trust you. You do that by creating win/win relationships.

The top 4 major social media sites right now are <u>Facebook</u>, <u>Twitter</u>, <u>LinkedIn</u> and <u>YouTube</u>. All of these **FREE** sites lets you profile yourself and your business and gives you the opportunity to connect with thousands if not millions of potential consumers of your products and services. In the interest of total transparency, at the time of this writing, I have yet to get on Twitter but I plan to change that in the coming weeks.

I believe the key to using social media successfully is authenticity. You are selling you. The real you, not some hyped up, fake version of you. Your authentic self is your attracting factor, you are branding yourself. So put your best foot forward.

It's important that in addition to being authentic, you portray a professional image online as well. A great way to do that on Facebook is to customize your business page with features your "Liker's" might find on your website. You can add video's, customize welcome tabs and add email sign up boxes among other things to your Facebook page. I found a great resource that makes this so easy. I use <u>FanPageEngine.com</u> and you can too. I bought the program for less than $70 bucks and it's a Godsend for technically challenged rookies like me =) <u>Create your own customized Facebook page at FanPageEngine.com</u>

PERSONAL GROWTH POWERHOUSES TO CHECK OUT

I love learning. And, whenever I come across great information that resonates with me I want to share it. The following is a very short list of experts who I have the utmost respect and whose work has helped me to understand and integrate universal principles and personal growth theory into the fabric of my life... I highly recommend you check them out. Of course, there are many many more books and people who have made a lasting impression on me, this is a short list.

FranklinCovey f/k/a Franklin Quest. This is where it all began for me. In 1996 this company came into my workplace and gave me the gift of "access" to personal growth information cleverly disguised as a mandatory "professional development" course for management staff. I highly recommend that you read, The 7 Habits of Highly Effective People by its co-founder, Stephen Covey.

Marie Diamond. Marie Diamond is a featured teacher in the hit movie, The Secret. I went on her personal transformation 4 day retreat and workshop via Learning Strategies and attended her 6 week Inner Diamond Tele-Seminar with her top coach, Annette Rugolo. Both the retreat and the course without a doubt transformed my energy and changed my life, literally. The information you receive from her will blow your mind! Connecting with her and her information is a must if you are at all attracted to accelerating your spiritual growth. She has some of the best information I've found on inner transformation and Feng Shui - how to enhance your environment so that it is a true reflection of you and what you want to accomplish. Download her Free E-Book and get your personal Law of Attraction number.

http://www.mariediamond.com/cmd.php?af=1152862

T Harv Eker. I love Harv Eker and his book, The Secrets of the Millionaire Mind and The Millionaire Mind Intensive (MMI) Workshop, presented by Peak Potentials. Both the book and the workshop has had a profound affect on my life and my confidence. Change your money blueprint (like I did) in one weekend and claim your financial freedom. I highly encourage you to buy the book and go to the seminar. I loved my experience at the workshop so much that I became an official affiliate of Peak Potentials. Here's access to an introductory tele-seminar. Just click this link and you will be on your way!

http://www.millionairemind.com/a/?wid=743566&page=/preview/replay

Jack Canfield. I attended Jack's Success Principle's Workshop in 2009. I left the workshop with my "Breakthrough Goal" to write a book. Make Life Work: Personal Growth For Today's Entrepreneur is complete! Jack is the co-creator of the billion dollar, Chicken Soup for the Soul book series and was featured in the The Secret. Get the Success Principles and sign up for his newsletter at www.jackcanfield.com or www.thesuccessprinciples.com.

The Secret. A movie by Rhonda Bryn. The Secret gives people a very good introduction to the universal law of *like attracts like* aka the *Law of Attraction*. Be sure to check out The Secret Summary by Bob

<u>Proctor</u> found in the Special Features section. Watch that over and over and over again. You may also want to read the book, The Secret for more in-depth understanding of how the law of attraction works.

<u>Abraham-Hicks. Esther and Jerry Hicks.</u> I cannot say enough about Abraham-Hicks! You should read anything you can put your hands on from them. One of the books that has helped me to understand the laws of the universe, myself and my relationship with life is their book, <u>The Vortex: Where the Law of Attraction Assembles All Cooperative Relationships</u>. Just go with it - their work is a must have! Visit their website, <u>www.abraham-hicks.com</u>.

RESOURCES – ARTICLE I

The Language of You by Gemeem Davis

The most important conversation you will ever have is the one between you and You. The you that sees, smells, tastes, touches and hears (the here and now you) and the You that exists inside of you. Call the *"Within You"* whatever you like - life, consciousness, spirit, higher self, your subconscious mind... you know where I'm going with this yes? Yes.

I call the process of communicating between you and You, *The Great Conversation* and there are two things you need to know to master it. The first thing is its language and the second is that it never stops. As long as you have a body and are breathing (and perhaps beyond that) you are engaged with it.

The language used in The Great Conversation and thus the Language of Life (You) is your feelings. You access your feelings with your thoughts. That is why there is such high regard for "thoughts" and "positive thinking" in self-help material. Advocating it is an attempt to get you into the realm of better *Feeling Thoughts*.

Despite the attempt, positive thinking is still one of the most misunderstood aspects of personal growth. Here's the fundamental problem. When we consider the phrase "positive thinking" we think it's a one-step, self explanatory directive, "just think positive thoughts and you'll get everything you want". Sounds good right? However in my experience and those of thousands who've tried and failed, "positive thinking" is a grossly over simplified misnomer. Instead of thinking positive we'd do better focusing our energy on "Believing Positive".

Belief is where it's at. Thinking is overrated.

Let's face it. You can think something all day long, you can even know it intellectually but if it hasn't been recognized by the *Within You* and become an integral part of how you operate, you don't really believe it. Therefore whatever you are trying to affect with your thinking will remain unaffected. The communication between you and You is off. When you believe something you have an emotional / feeling connection to the object of your belief and you act in accordance with it.

Getting to *Believing Positive* is the only place you need to go to set yourself up for success. You get there through repetition. This is because, by nature we are habitual beings. This is why the practice of creating and repeating affirmations is such a popular tool for accelerating personal growth. With new, effective, power-filled affirmations you bypass your old programmed thinking, and "set" the *Within You* on the course of your choosing.

Using affirmations to get to your Believing.

An affirmation is a declaration that something is true. It matters not what you are affirming. Right or wrong, if you affirm something long enough or passionately enough it will become a part of your *Within*

You programing, and evidence of it will show up in your life. When working with affirmations, keep the following in mind:

- Great affirmations elicit strong emotions.
- Write them in the present tense.
- Be positive.
- Keep it brief.
- Use verbs - include "action" words.
- Repeat them as much as possible throughout the day.

Use affirmations to master the *The Great Conversation*. Remember the *Language of You (Life)* are your feelings. You access your feelings with your thoughts. Your thoughts determine your action and you actions deliver your results. Every time.

Practically speaking, you can think of affirmations as abbreviated versions of your goals, so consider creating one for each thing you want to accomplish and every aspect of your life that you want to change.

RESOURCES – ARTICLE II

Bring Only What You Love by Gemeem Davis

Your awareness will determine whether you're "successful". It took me about ten years of looking for the secret to success in processes like goal setting and time management before I realized that it was how I looked at and felt about my past experiences and current circumstances that was determining my level of success.

When I was in my mid-twenties I hated my job. I worked for a large national bank in a branch office in Center-City, Philadelphia. I was responsible for hundreds of thousands of dollars, had keys to the branch, the combination to the vault and had received my first professional award. I even had the privilege of attending one of the most popular and successful professional development/management training programs in the country. But if you would have asked me back then if I thought of myself as successful, more than likely I would have broke down in tears and told you how unsuccessful I felt because I wasn't making "x" amount of dollars, hadn't completed my college education and that I was consumed with fear about the possibility of not making it out of my "dead-end" job, even though I had been promoted three times!

I couldn't see for looking. All I saw was what I did not want. I did not want to be a worker-bee stuck in a traditional 9 to 5, I did not want to be broke. I did not want to appear ignorant and uneducated. I was so focused, so aware of what I did not want, that it "what I did not want", became the dominant yet unconscious point from which I made decisions, did all my asking (ok, really, all my "Lord please" begging) and the place where I held my true intentions, hostage. Although, I didn't know it at the time, I was actually developing a *Pattern of Awareness*, a mindset, a way of seeing that was rooted in lack.

Because that was my mindset receiving what *I did not want* became the experience that played itself out in every aspect of my life. I didn't want to be broke… I struggled financially. I didn't want to be a worker-bee…I attracted low-level jobs where I had to work hard and prove myself. I didn't want to be alone…my romantic relationships failed and my friendships were in turmoil. I wasn't succeeding at anything… or so I thought.

After years of struggle and trying to figure out why I wasn't moving forward, I had a breakthrough. While packing to move to a new apartment I had this thought, *"Bring only what you love"*.

Obeying the directive I made three piles, things to keep, things to give away and things to throw out. In the things to keep pile (which contained only things I loved and regarded as valuable) I had placed an award I received while working at the bank, a newspaper clipping of the Debutante Cotillion I attended when I was in high school, a recognition award for volunteering, my college degree (which I had received five years earlier) and the Certificate of Excellence award I received upon graduation.

Surrounded by my things to keep, the things I loved, I began to see my past and myself in a new light. I recognized that there was more to my life than my perception of failure and apparent lack. There, amongst my things, was a thread, a pattern of excellence weaving its way through my life experiences that I had previously been blind to.

Immediately I began to feel good and proud about where I had been, what I've done and who I was. I could feel my energy shifting, becoming lighter, more relaxed and confident in my ability to achieve excellence and experience "success". After all I had done it before and didn't even know it.

"Imagine what I could do when consciously creating" I thought.

When I got to my new apartment I wanted to remind myself of the excellence and success in my past so I created a "Wall of Success". I hung my awards, the newspaper clipping, degrees etc. above my desk. I spend a little time focusing my attention on my "Wall of Success" everyday. So now, when I sit down to do work, I am conscious of the fact that I am building on the success I already have, *bringing only what I love* to my present moments and future endeavors.

What are you bringing to your present and future moments? Sift through your things, find items you love and that make you feel good and proud about who you are. Place them where you can see them.

Create a "Wall of Success" in your home and/or office. I guarantee that by focusing your attention in the direction of your success, your energy will change, you will feel better and create more of what you want and less of what you don't want.

RESOURCES – ARTICLE III

The Having Space by Gemeem Davis

Naturally, at the start of a new year people feel a sense of renewal and hope that what's in front of them will be better than what's behind them. Resolutions are made and goals are set in an attempt to bottle that hope and realize long held desires.

Unfortunately for many people, the sense of hope and energy surrounding the new year quickly fades into everyday life. Resolutions fall by the wayside and goals go unfulfilled, pushed into a mysterious future. This process of *wanting yet not receiving*, is repeated by millions year after year after year. Why?

During his campaign for the Presidency for the United States, Barack Obama reminded us of one of Albert Einstein's most famous statements, "The definition of insanity is doing the same thing over and over again expecting a different result." So does that mean that the millions of people who make resolutions and struggle with the same goals (to lose weight, make more money, save more money and take a vacation, etc.) year after year are insane? Perhaps. But, rather than diagnose ninety-eight percent of the world's population with a mental illness (besides, I'm not a psychologist), I'm inclined to believe that the key to understanding why people repeatedly activate the *wanting yet not receiving energy* in their lives, lies in understanding our habitual nature.

Life happens automatically. Day in and day out our bodies perform a plethora of tasks like breathing, moving a limb, circulating blood, digesting food and talking without us having to consciously think about it. A "habit" by definition is nothing more than unconscious repetitive actions or behavior. Our bodies "natural habits" were developed to serve our greatest good. Can you imagine what it would be like if we had to consciously think about how to breathe every second of every minute of every day? You'd never get anything done. You'd be too busy trying to stay alive!

Our daily thoughts (most of them anyway) are also on automatic. And, that's a good thing, especially if you consistently feel good about who and where you are. However, habitual thoughts may hinder you if you want *change* in your life. Think about it, if thoughts determine your actions and your actions determine your results, then, the thoughts you've been thinking up until now have gotten you exactly where you are, to *the place where you're asking for change.* To experience something new in any area of your life, it's imperative to replace old thought habits with new ones that support what you are seeking.

Are habitual thoughts about goal setting and success supporting or hindering you?

If you ask any good "personal success" expert, coach or trainer, what the first step to the successful achievement of anything is, I guarantee you that he or she will tell you that *step one is to get clear.* The protocol for doing that is to decide what you want by asking yourself, *what do I want?* The answers you come up with usually result in a long list of things you want to have, do and be. Your list then serves as proof of your *wanting*.

There's only one problem. If you've been struggling to achieve the things on your *I Want List* year after year, you can reasonably conclude that there is a flaw somewhere in your thinking. Remember, your thoughts are the root cause of everything you experience. Perhaps it is time to give up the *I Want Asking Approach* to getting clear and setting goals all together.

Change your approach. Enter *The Having Space.*

"I Want" is a habit. Replace it with "What do I have to give?"

A few years ago I needed money, badly. So I did what any independent thirty-something would do in a crisis. I called my mother! After about an hour listening to me cry about everything wrong in my life, she did her mom thing and gave me a really good practical solution, "you should register with a temporary employment agency". I did and my cash flow improved. But the most valuable thing I received from my work was not money. It was an idea.

The last company I worked for was going through major changes. As a result, they hired a corporate trainer to come in and ease the employees into a new culture of accountability, commitment and integrity. During a mandatory training session on how employees would be evaluated, the trainer made a statement that had a profound effect on my life. In her very relaxed yet powerful voice she said, *"We expect you to give us your best"*. I not only heard those words, I felt them. I went back to my desk knowing a shift had occurred, my awareness opened up. All I could think about for the rest of the day was "what's my best?" By five o'clock I had my answer. It was time to stop playing small (in the accounting department) and offer my interests, passion, professional skill and propensity to communicate, to the employer I thought of as temporary. Two months later I had created a professional development workshop program I called, Make Work (Work): Strategic Planning For Every Employee, proposed it to the Director of Training and Development and made the decision to start a consulting and personal development training company of my own.

What happened? What was the shift? How was it that I was able to turn inspiring words into a tangible product and service and find the courage to propose it to corporate executives who had no idea that I had a background in professional development? Where did the audacity, confidence and commitment to follow through on *my best* come from that told me yes. Yes you can own a business even though you've never done anything like that before?

The best way I can explain it is to say that, in my contemplation of what was my best and how I could *give that* to my co-workers and employer, *I stopped asking for what I wanted.* Instead of being behind my goals trying to figure them out, I went to the place where they found me, my *Having Space*, where *All That Is* already exists. Where what was mine, *what I already had*, which were my interests, passion, talents, skills and authentic voice was enough.

The Having Space is where I am enough. And, so are you. Enter it NOW.

THANK YOU!

Wow! I am so happy, grateful and honored that we are connected. I knew you were here, trying to figure it all out; the Law of Attraction, Goal Setting, the principles of success, how to start your business. I know how it feels to want, to be confused, to be hit with so much information on the Internet that you forget why you turned your computer on in the first place. So I humbly thank you for allowing me and <u>Make Life Work</u> into your life. I trust that you've found the information here compelling and beneficial and that it has exceeded your expectations.

Thank You, Thank You, Thank You!

And please, email me at <u>gemeem@makelifeworknow.com</u> with any questions. I read my own email and will do my very best to answer every question personally.

ABOUT THE AUTHOR

Gemeem Davis was first introduced to professional development in 1996 through a management/leadership training program offered to her through her job for a large national bank. Recognizing the power of the information, *to move her from where she was to where she really wanted to be*, she made a promise to herself to *work* the information in her own life, then find a way to bring the process of change - clarity, choice and action to people who traditionally lack access to learned business skills.

In 2003, Gemeem made her first major steps in that direction, when she began coordinating one of the most innovative and successful professional development programs for artists in North America. The program, at The Creative Capital Foundation has reached more than fifteen hundred artists in every discipline across The United States and Great Britain.

Her mission is to empower people all around the world to live and work on their own terms.

Stay connected with Gemeem on Facebook and at www.makelifeworknow.com, there you'll find out how to attend a live Make Life Work workshop or participate in a 4-Week Make Life Work Tele-Seminar.

www.ingramcontent.com/pod-product-compliance
Lightning Source LLC
Chambersburg PA
CBHW051541170526
45165CB00002B/833